Katrin Behren

Indoor Cats

Filled with Full-color Photographs
Illustrated by Renate Holzner

BARRON'S

CONTENTS

T Y P I C A L
INDOOR CATS

- Soft fur
- Sharp teeth and claws
- Many distinct breeds and colors, with long or short hair
- Affectionate cuddlers
- Fierce predators
- Able to see in the dark
- Excellent climbers and gymnasts
- Independent and aloof
- March to their own drummer

When wild, tawny African cats were lured into contact with humans by the rats and mice that threatened the granaries in Egypt around 1500 B.C., something extraordinary happened. The cat domesticated itself. For that reason, people worshipped the cat as the goddess Bastet, represented as a woman with a cat's head.

But then cats fell on hard times. Their popularity waned until the eighteenth century, when their rise to the status of beloved house pets began.

CHOOSING A CAT

1 Mixed breed or pure-bred? The difference is not just in appearance and price, but in character and behavior as well (see The Right Cat for You, page 9).

2 Indoor cats can live to be 15 years or older. That's how long you'll be responsible for your pet.

3 Male and female cats are equally affectionate. Pet cats should be neutered or spayed (see page 24).

4 If you are a single working person, consider getting two cats (see page 12).

5 Do you have any house pets that might not be compatible with a cat (see page 16)?

6 If you want an old, established cat and a new kitten to get along with one another, you must proceed cautiously (see page 12).

7 If you give your child a cat as a playmate, you should still keep an eye on both of them (see page 32).

8 Who will take care of your cat while you're on vacation or if you're sick?

9 If you regularly go to a vacation home, your cat will become accustomed to the second home (see page 30).

Is a Cat for You?

A cat can adapt to any household. Just the same, you should understand a few things before getting a cat. You'll be dealing with a strong-willed personality over the course of several years.

Singles: Independent people structure their lives differently from people who have a family. So before you get a cat, consider whether owning a cat fits in with your plans for the future. What happens if a partner comes along who doesn't like the cat? Or if you have to travel for your job, or leave for vacation?

Older people: Cats are very comforting for older people. They are a consolation in solitude, and are easy to care for. But what do you do if you want to take a vacation or have to go to the hospital?

Note: If you take in an older cat, for example one from an animal shelter (see page 10), you won't have to be responsible for it for as many years as you would for a kitten.

Families: Cats can get used to even the most turbulent households, unless you're dealing with a particularly nervous kind of cat. You'll have to determine who will care for the cat, feed it regularly, and clean out the litterbox.

CHOOSING A CAT AND BRINGING IT HOME

Gracefulness, affectionate nature, soft fur, contented purring whenever they snuggle in their owner's lap—these are some of the reasons people love cats and enjoy living with them.

Indoor Cats

Cats are independent, but they prefer the company of humans. As people have occupied more and more apartments in the course of urbanization, cats have tagged along. Unfortunately, living in a city is full of dangers for cats, so people have protected them by keeping them in their homes. Cats have adapted without abandoning their independent nature.

Let's consider for a moment a cat's daily life. Cats spend most of the day either sleeping or resting. When they're awake, they sharpen their claws, look for hiding places, explore their territory, satisfy their hunger, and socialize whenever they feel like it. As long as we make it possible for kitty to pursue all these activities within the confines of our four walls, it will nestle right in at home with no trouble at all.

A home with assorted nooks to hide in, a scenic overlook from a window or a balcony, some toys to play with, and your loving care and attention will make your cat happy and comfortable. And an indoor cat can lead a

A box filled with tissue paper is an inexpensive toy for a playful kitten.

longer and safer life than a cat that is allowed to come and go inside and out.

Missing Freedom

The big question is whether cats that aren't allowed to run free miss their freedom. In my opinion, if they never have been allowed to run free from the time they were small, they have not developed a taste for it. In fact, they feel overwhelmed if they occasionally get out into nature. It's different if they regularly get to run free on the weekend or on vacation. Cats adjust very quickly to situations that become routine.

The Right Cat for You

Kittens: You can get kittens from friends or neighbors, or through a notice at a pet shop. Check out a kitten thoroughly so that you choose one that suits you best (see page 13). Lots of things affect a kitten's character. For example, if the mother cat is friendly with humans, that gets impressed upon her kittens. Watch how the kittens sort things out at the "milk bar," how they play with one another, if they have figured out how to use the litterbox, and whether they are receptive to strangers or tuck tail and hide from them.

Purebred cats: Sometimes people fall in love with a particular type of purebred, based mostly on appearance. But that shouldn't be the only consideration. Purebreds are not inexpensive, so you should first find out if that breed is suited to your needs (see page 14). It's best to buy from a breeder (see Addresses, page 62) or from a reputable pet store. Also get the pedigree, shot record, and a sales agreement, and find out if the kitten has been wormed (see page 53).

Animal Shelters: Homeless cats are given away by animal shelters, humane societies, or cat rescue organizations. The purchase price may not include having the cat inoculated, wormed, and neutered. Only cats that have

A kitten bonds very closely with its mother and siblings.

already lived with people are suitable for indoor living.

Newspaper Ads: Ads in the classified section of a newspaper may or may not be a good place to find a cat. There are cat fanciers who are truly concerned only with finding good accommodations for the cat. Many give the kittens away free; others charge money because they have already had the kittens immunized and wormed, and they want to recover their costs. In addition, there are the wheelers and dealers who want their cats to have litters as often as possible just to make money. Usually these cats have not been vaccinated when they go up for sale. Often owners of purebred cats advertise so-called fanciers' cats for sale, just as professional breeders do.

Cats from a Pet Shop: Responsible pet shop owners keep their cats clean, provide them with opportunities to play and cuddle, and give them necessary attention. In addition, they will give you good advice on choosing a kitten.

Stray Cats: Sometimes you may find homeless wanderers when you're on vacation. When you feel pangs of sympathy for these strays, just remember that you know nothing about the origins of such animals, what diseases or parasites they might be carrying, or even if they will be able to adapt to indoor living. And often bringing a cat home over long distances can be fraught with difficulties.

Male or Female?

A female cat becomes sexually mature between the sixth and twelfth month of life. Indoor cats subjected to artificial light and temperatures may cycle every two or three weeks for months at a time. Because she usually has no chance to connect with a male cat inside the home, she will remain in a mood for love much of the time.

A male cat becomes sexually mature at the age of nine months, and then begins to mark his territory by spraying urine in places. The stench is most unpleasant. You can eliminate this problem by having the animal neutered (see page 24).

Determining Sex in Kittens: The distance between a male's anus and penis is greater than the distance between a female's anus and vulva. In older cats, the difference is more obvious.

Checklist
Before You Get a Cat

1 Are you prepared to provide enough variety and activity for your cat so that living inside doesn't restrict its natural behavior?

2 Can you live with cat hair on your rugs, furniture, and clothes? Will you mind picking up hair balls that cats regurgitate onto the rugs or changing the litter in the cat's litterbox?

3 Do you understand that a cat needs to be vaccinated regularly? (See page 56.) Have you calculated the cost of veterinary care, feeding, and other expenses?

4 Have you talked things over with your landlord (see Tip, page 16)?

5 Are you or any family members allergic to cat hair?

One Cat or a Pair?

Many cats that have to spend the day alone while their owners are at work will find life boring. If two cats get along well, they will keep each other moving, play, cuddle, or spar with one another. Don't worry; they won't ignore you, and will come back to you whenever they feel like it.

Consider these possibilities if you want two cats:

✔ Two siblings from a litter

✔ An older and a younger cat, when the new arrival is able to adapt to the older, established cat

✔ Two grown cats; you'll need lots of patience to help them acclimate to one another, plus plenty of room in the home so that each can stake out its territory (see next paragraph).

Cat Meets Cat

It takes a fine touch to get an older cat to make friends with a new kitten. The older cat regards the home where it has so far reigned alone as its own property, and it will defend it tooth and claw. In the wild, the newcomer would respect that and withdraw. But that doesn't work in the house, so the older cat reacts defensively and as if it were insulted; it may stop eating, or defecate in the middle of the carpet in order to show its dominance. You can find out how to get two cats used to each other on page 32.

Note: Sometimes it's not the old cat that terrorizes the new one, but the reverse. If you can't resolve this problem, I recommend that you make other arrangements for the newcomer. After all, your old friend was there first.

Cats and Other House Pets

Cats will not be afraid of any animals that are smaller than they; rather, cats will regard them as playthings or prey. Animals that are as large or larger are considered enemies until the cat becomes convinced otherwise.

Dogs: If you already have a dog, there probably won't be many problems, unless the dog is already a cat-hater because of previous experience. The supposed instinctive antipathy between dogs and cats has little basis in reality.

Animosity between cats and dogs can be caused by their different body language. For example, tail wagging signifies readiness to make contact and a friendly mood in dogs; with cats, on the other hand, moving the tail indicates strained watchfulness, edginess, and aggressiveness. Dogs sniff each other under the tail when they get acquainted. Cats are more reserved by nature, and sniff each other nose to nose only after some time has gone by. They react to sudden attempts to get close, which they interpret as attacks, by spitting and lifting their paws in a threatening gesture. For dogs, that means, "Play with me!" And a dog will chase a running cat and try to catch it.

Siblings from a litter get along fine with one another for life.

What Kind of Cat Is Right for You?

Whether black, red, tabby, or exotic purebred, the cat's temperament is the key. The following descriptions and bits of advice should help you find the right cat. If your kitty turns out to be different, don't hold that against it. There are no precise recipes for such multifaceted creatures.

Temperament	How to Get Acquainted	Breeds with These Characteristics
A sociable cat comes up to you after holding back for a moment, lets you pet it and stroke its head. It's curious, active, and playful, and it connects easily with children.	Don't be too forceful. Wait until the cat willingly comes up to you to cuddle or play.	Maine Coon, Norwegian Forest Cat, Turkish Angora, Somali, Birman, Rag Doll, Scottish Fold, Manx
A calm cat is even-tempered and displays patience around its siblings. It takes its time in making contact, since it sniffs everything deliberately and won't be hurried.	Again, wait until the cat approaches you.	Persian, Exotic Shorthair
A shy cat withdraws to a corner and observes from there. Once the ice is broken, it bonds very closely with its human.	You can't rush this cat into doing anything. Use treats to show it that you're in charge; thus if the cat pleases you it will get a reward.	Various individuals, regardless of breed
An impulsive cat likes to be the center of attention and can sulk for hours if you ignore it. This very temperamental type of cat is dependent on people and needs lots of attention.	Such characteristics are usually peculiar to certain breeds. You have to take this into consideration before making a choice.	Abyssinian, Burmese, Oriental Shorthair, Rex, Russian Blue, Siamese

PORTRAITS:
INDOOR CATS

Purebred cats are different not only in appearance, but also in temperament. This consideration should always play a role in your choice of a housemate.

Siamese, lilac point—a breed that's very attuned to humans.

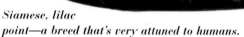

Above: British Shorthair, Blue or Carthusian. A delightful cat that also gets along well with other cats and house pets.

Above: British Shorthair, silver striped. This breed is even-tempered, self-assured, and ideally suited to indoor living.

Left: The Maine Coon, here in the silver tabby color, loves exercise on the porch.

Left: The Burmese has a self-assured personality.

Below: Abyssinian; this breed needs lots of care and attention.

Right: Somali; by nature very playful, lively, affectionate, and extremely friendly.

Birman, seal point. Well suited to a family with children.

Above: Persian, chinchilla; an affectionate, sociable, and friendly cat.

TIP

Legal Considerations

Renting: When renting an apartment, you must check with the landlord to see if cats are allowed.

Condominiums: Usually cat ownership can be prohibited only by a resolution passed by the condominium owners.

Running Free: For cats, running free is part of their nature. But a cat that has been kept indoors from the beginning will be perfectly content.

Pet Owner's Liability Insurance: Pet owners are liable for damages that their cats cause to people or property.

Purchase Agreement: Although an oral purchase agreement is binding, it is recommended that you obtain a receipt from the seller, or, in the case of valuable purebred cats, that a contract be written and signed by you and the breeder. Reputable breeders will insist upon this. In case a defect or illness is detected after buying the cat, the purchase can be rescinded, or the purchase price reduced, provided that the cat was already sick before ownership was transferred.

Read before You Sign: Make sure you understand all terms of the contract before you sign. Health records and vaccination certificates should accompany the purchase agreement. Some breeders vaccinate their own kittens, which is a legal practice.

Things can go smoothly when two animals are kept together from the time they are small, or when a young kitten joins a grown dog. But you have to train them to accept one another, and you shouldn't just leave the two of them to their own devices (see page 32). There may be problems if a self-assured adult cat that likes to be the center of attention is confronted with a young puppy. The cat can play lord over the dog to the point that the latter becomes a fearful, unhappy creature that wants only to hide.

Guinea Pigs and Hamsters: Cats can make friends with guinea pigs, but you shouldn't count on it. Cats will consider hamsters prey.

Dwarf Rabbits: Cats will regard these pets as prey. Keep them in separate rooms, or the rabbit will be terrified.

Budgies and Canaries: Cats do hunt birds, although sometimes they can become friends; don't count on it!

Parrots and Larger Parakeets: They may become jealous, and can hurt the cat with their beaks; cats may paw or bite the birds. Keep them apart.

Choosing the Right Kitten

When you look for a kitten, don't consider only how sweet they look; check to see how contented they are, and especially what their behavior is like.

Kittens play and tumble a lot. Then they take a snooze break, often without any transition from play. They are cautious with unknown people, but curious and interested. So observe how they go to their owner, and whether they play with that person and let themselves get caught. That kind of cat is used to people, and it will provide you with lots of pleasure. If the kitten merely slinks away, and doesn't even let trusted people stroke it, that's an animal only for an experienced cat owner.

A cat that sits around on the sidelines and is apathetic might be sick. In contrast, signs of a healthy cat are:

✔ The fur feels thick and soft, and never unkempt (although kitten fur is not as smooth and shiny as the coat of an adult cat).

✔ The eyes are clear and shiny; they must be free of tears and any kind of abnormality.

✔ The nose is dry and warm, but not hot.

✔ The ears move in reaction to every noise in the surroundings. The insides are clean. Shaking the head or holding it at an angle are signs of an ear infection.

✔ The anal region must be clean, not dirty or matted.

✔ The belly must not be fat or distended, because this might indicate an infestation of worms.

✔ The kitten's body should be well padded all around and not feel light as a feather when you pick it up.

Everything a Cat Needs

You should have the following things on hand and already set up in the appropriate place when your cat comes home. That way the cat can sniff them and get used to them as soon as it makes its first explorations.

✔ *A Cat Bed:* A basket, either open or with a roof, is essential to every cat. It doesn't have to be thickly padded; a piece of soft fabric is adequate.

✔ *A Litterbox:* Pet shops offer three versions:
- A simple plastic pan; it's also good for traveling.
- A plastic pan with a raised rim to keep the litter from flying out.
- An enclosed litterbox with a drawer— the cleanest arrangement since some cats urinate while standing.

You also need:

✔ *Litter:* It is very effective in reducing odors. It must be guaranteed free of asbestos (read the label!). It's usually available in bags of 2 to 20 pounds (4–50 kg). Pet stores carry a type of litter that's economical to use, since the droppings form clumps that can be removed with a plastic shovel and disposed of.

Dogs and cats can become the best of friends if they grow up together.

Note: In some places you may be able to have litter and cat food delivered directly to your door. You could inquire about this at your pet store.

Climbing Tree and Scratching Board: You need a climbing tree or a scratching board so that your cat doesn't claw rugs, carpets, or upholstered furniture (see HOW-TO: Living Space, pages 26–27).

Food and Water Dishes: You'll need one to two food dishes for each cat (for fresh and dry food), plus a water dish. The cat doesn't care what the dishes are made of or what they look like, but they must be solid so they don't go rolling through the house if the cat licks them clean with too much gusto.

There's a fine view of the whole territory from a comfortable vantage point like this one.

Cat Grass: Cats need greens to help them regurgitate the hairs they swallow when they groom themselves. To prevent hairballs, get them used to the specific grass that's designed for them (from the pet store), because many houseplants are toxic to them (see TIP: Nibbling on Plants, page 46).

In addition to providing cat grass, dab some plain petroleum jelly on your cat's paw to lick off. This will help your pet expel hairballs.

Self Feeders

Many cat owners prefer to offer dry food free-choice for their cats to nibble on throughout the day. Self-feeders handily dispense food from a bulk hopper as the cat eats. The food usually lasts a few days, making the feeders convenient when you're away overnight or for a weekend. Your pet store also carries self-waterers that dispense water from an inverted bottle into a dish as the cat drinks. Of course, there's always the possibility that your creative cat will regard these objects as playthings, shoveling out kibble or splashing water with its paws simply to watch a food shower or a waterfall.

Cat Toys

Your pet store offers a variety of cat toys, including the catnip-stuffed variety that most cats love. In addition, you can create inexpensive playthings to keep your cat from becoming bored. Make a fascinating rolling rattle by putting a marble in an empty plastic film case and sealing the case securely with duct tape. Cats also love empty thread spools and wadded-up pieces of paper. Recycle your tennis balls or golf balls. Cut peepholes in empty boxes, or tape boxes together to form a tunnel. Securely sew felt ears on discarded shoulder pads from last year's clothes to make little mousies.

Never let your cat play with small items it could choke on, such as buttons, paper clips, hair ornaments, and rubber bands. Keep on eye on your pet when it plays with flexible, fishing-pole-type toys with feathers, sequins, or other items that whiz through the air and might fly off. Put these toys away when you cannot be in the room with kitty. Don't let your pet play with balloons, which will inevitably pop, leaving strings of plastic your cat could chew and choke on, or which could cause a fatal intestinal blockage.

Checklist
Accessories

1 A willow basket or a soft cubby hole to sleep in.

2 A litterbox with a raised rim, or an enclosed litterbox with a drawer.

3 Litter, guaranteed to be asbestos-free and odor-inhibiting.

4 A scratching tree for climbing, playing, and sleeping, or a scratching board.

5 A comb and brush for taking care of longhaired cats.

6 Food and water dishes, preferably thick-walled and stable.

7 Cat grass, which aids in regurgitating hair swallowed while grooming.

8 Toys, for example a stuffed mouse or a mouse pull-toy, all types of balls, stuffed animals on a wooden dowel, empty thread spools, small animal on flexible wire, and many more.

The Trip Home

A basket or a plastic travel cage makes an acceptable transportation container. Two people should drive to pick up the cat. That way one person can speak reassuringly to the cat during the ride home. Once home, place the container in the room you want the cat to get to know first, and then open the door.

It's easy to carry a cat on any kind of trip in a plastic travel crate or kennel.

Acclimating a Young Cat

✔ At first let the kitten run around in just one room. In the same room, put the litterbox, a small dish of the food that the cat is used to, and a dish of water.

✔ Crouch beside the basket and get the animal's attention by calling its name. It will no doubt meow to call to its mother and siblings. Answer it with a soft voice so it can get used to you.

✔ Soon the kitten will have enough courage to venture forth curiously and have a look at its new home. It will creep carefully along the walls on its belly, hide under a sofa, an armchair, or a cupboard, and it won't want to come out.

In these first hours and days, don't leave the kitten alone any more than necessary. The bonding between kitten and mother and siblings is very close. You have to make up for the little one's loss. Stroke it, pet it, and play with it.

Note: Always be aware that kittens run trustingly between your feet and rub you with their head, try to climb up on you, and have no idea that they can be stepped on or crushed in a closing door. So always be careful in closing doors. The little creatures can easily get into trouble, so you have to be watchful at all times.

If you work or play games at a computer, allow your kitten to sit by the screen. Kittens are endlessly fascinated by the moving cursor and action-packed computer games.

The kitten takes the first step in investigating its new home.

Getting Used to a New Person

It can be difficult for a cat to get used to living with a new person after it's lived with another one for many years. It has been so attached to its previous owner that it's consumed with homesickness and grief. Large doses of love and tenderness will help the cat bond with you. Some cats settle in quickly. Others take longer to feel at home. It helps if your house is quiet and there aren't other pets to add to the newcomer's stress.

Acclimating an Older Cat

In theory, the process of acclimating an older cat should be about the same as with a young kitten. But since the cat has already imprinted in its old surroundings, you have to take that into account and proceed deliberately.

The Fearful Cat: Perhaps it's had some bad experiences with people. Try to find out what it's afraid of. That might be movement, noises, or lots of hubbub in the family. Use no force, and always leave the cat a chance to retreat to a quiet place. It needs calm and must not be frightened. That would only make it more withdrawn.

The Problem Cat: You got it from the humane society, and it bites and scratches you when you try to catch it. Love and patience are the only solution. Don't chase it; feed it regularly, and be calm and relaxed. Gradually it will get to know you and become friendly.

Free Exercise

If you want to give your feline friend a little fresh air from time to time you should get it used to a leash. That not only makes a walk safe, but is also convenient for trips to the veterinarian (see page 55). Pet stores sell special cat leashes with chest harnesses. Here's how to proceed:

Getting the Cat Used to a Leash and Harness: Let the cat play with them for a few days. Then put the harness on for a little longer each time.

Getting it Used to the Tension: Clip on the leash and lure the cat with a treat so that it walks forward. Praise it and stroke it if that works.

The harness around the chest and belly hardly cramps the cat.

Walking on a Leash: Lead the cat around inside the home without using treats until it goes without balking. Don't forget to pet and praise.

Now kitty is ready for the first trip outside.

Treats are used to encourage the cat to walk with a leash.

LIVING WITH A CAT

Be nice to your cat and it will delight you
with its incomparable personality
and reward you with life-long devotion.

Arranging Your Home for Your Cat

It's easy to set up a home that cats will like. It doesn't cost much money, and you don't have to compromise your requirements for comfort in order to offer your new housemate what it needs to feel at ease.

The home is as much a territory for the cat as the outdoors would be. As soon as it has settled in, a cat regards the home as its personal property that it willingly shares with the human occupants. It has selected several secure resting places, of which it considers itself sole proprietor. Among them is one place that the cat literally lives in. It is the calm refuge in its life, usually a room, but perhaps just a preferred spot where it spends several hours every day. In the rest of the home the cat roams about, meets the other inhabitants, and searches for hiding places.

Space Requirements

In order to provide the cat with as much variety, exercise, and freedom as possible, the home should be set up like a natural habitat. From the cat's point of view, variety is a source

Pointed ears and intense gaze are signs
of heightened alertness.

of stimulation; of course, dangers should be eliminated (see page 28).

One-room Apartments: A single room where the cat can observe everything from one place without moving becomes boring and monotonous after a while. Expand vertically by providing elevated seats on cupboards and shelves, or a climbing tree. Cats also love to look out windows.

Apartments with Several Rooms: Several rooms, including kitchen and bath, can always be explored. There should be no areas that are off limits; that is, kitty should have access to all rooms. The cat needs to patrol its territory countless times every day. It repeats these inspection tours at short intervals, but you'll regret it if its way is barred by doors. It will sit in front of them and meow persistently, and if they don't open, it will scratch and paw at them.

Opportunities to Scratch

Cats need a chance to scratch for several reasons. When scratching, they exercise the mechanism that extends and retracts the claws, demonstrate superiority, work off frustration and anger, and mark their territory. When the cat scratches a post, it peels the outer layer from its retractile claws. It also marks the post when

TIP

Neutering and Spaying

Neutering includes surgical removal of the testicles. Spaying, a more expensive procedure, involves opening the female's abdomen and removing the uterus, tubes, and ovaries. A female cat can be spayed from the age of six months on; a male cat can be neutered after it reaches sexual maturity when it's about a year old. The operation can be done under general anesthesia by any veterinarian. Usually the cat can be brought home soon afterward.

Both operations reduce cats' natural inclination to roam, particularly in search of sexual encounters. Neutering curbs a male's desire to spray in the house, marking his territory. Your cat will be healthier, too. Neutering the male eliminates testicular disease and decreases the chance of prostate cancer in later life. Spaying the female reduces her chances of contracting breast cancer and eliminates the possibility of her becoming pregnant.

If cost concerns you, ask your local animal shelter or veterinarian about low-cost spay and neuter programs in your area. Shelters sometimes work in cooperation with veterinarians to sponsor "Spay and Neuter Days," and invite cat owners to contribute whatever they can afford.

the scent glands on the underside of the front paws rub against the post. And if a cat lives with another cat that has visited the spot in the meantime, it will enthusiastically work over the scratching post in order to mark it. You can see how important a scratching post is; without it, the cat will misappropriate your furnishings.

Sleeping Places

It doesn't matter to the cat if it has a basket or a cardboard box. The main thing is that it be located in a warm spot. Now, whether kitty actually spends the night there may be another question entirely. It may want to curl up on your bed. In order to get the cat used to its own place, you have to be exceptionally persistent.

Litterbox

Cats bury their droppings, not so much for reasons of cleanliness as for a way to show their rank. Dominant cats in the wild leave their droppings uncovered in the most conspicuous places as a scent threat. Friendly or subordinate cats, on the other hand, bury their droppings. They continue to do this when they live with humans, provided that their life together is harmonious and undisturbed. You'll find some useful information about this in the HOW-TO on page 26.

This cat is pretending the ball is a mouse. It swats it so it rolls then pounces on it.

Exercise on the Balcony

An indoor cat whose territory extends to the balcony or a roof terrace can consider itself fortunate. Here it has fresh air and sunshine, as well as opportunities to search out various observation posts, according to its mood and desire. It must continually choose between sun and shade, and must be able to get back inside when it wishes.

Consider the following points:

✔ Securing the balcony: To keep the cat from falling accidentally, you have to secure your balcony, for example with sturdy turkey wire. That protects the cat without obstructing its view. Some landlords don't permit such measures. Find out first. Of course, accidents could still occur.

✔ Securing the roof terrace: In addition to the danger of falling, there's a possibility of

Cats prefer to take over the armchair where you like to sit.

conflict with the neighbors if kitty strolls across the roof and enters someone else's apartment. It's best to have your cat on a leash when sunning on the roof's "tar beach."

✔ Set-up: If space allows, you can set up a natural scratching and climbing tree with lookout places. Provide a rest area between window boxes, and a container with cat grass so that kitty doesn't attack your plants (see Making Your Home Safe for a Cat, page 28).

✔ Cat door: With a cat door, you don't have to leave the door to the balcony or a window open, and kitty can wander back and forth whenever it wants.

Here's how to set up a home so a cat will like it. The tips are intended as suggestions and should help you find appropriate solutions for your home. If you rent, check your lease to be sure you can makes these changes.

Lookouts on Windowsill and Balcony

Windowsills that are too narrow can be widened

to make room for a pot of cat grass as well as the cat. A sitting place can be set up on the balcony with a board at chest height. Of course the balcony has to be secured (see page 25), since even the cleverest cat can take a fall if it leaps at a bird fluttering by.

Litterbox

Location: In a quiet, protected place where the cat is unobserved, for example in the bathroom. There the floor is usually tiled and easy to clean. Kitty must always have access to it.

Note: The litterbox should never be placed near the food dishes, since that would be unsanitary and would interfere with the cat's eating.

Cleaning: Put between 1 and 2 inches (3–4 cm) of litter in the litterbox. Remove droppings and wet litter every day and pour in a little fresh litter (see Litter, page 17).

Cat Trail

A cat trail that your tame tiger can easily climb up and down can be incorporated into practically any type of home decor. Pet stores sell climbing apparatus that can be attached to the walls on an angle with brackets. Lookouts and lairs complete the climbing area. You

Cats like to observe their domain from on high, so build ramps and ladders for them to climb.

Once a week put all the litter into a plastic bag and throw it away. Don't dispose of it in the toilet. Rinse out the litterbox with hot water. Don't use any soaps or disinfectants, since cats don't like the smell and may abandon the litterbox. Wipe it dry and fill with fresh litter.

Note: If two cats use the litterbox, they visit it more frequently, because one keeps marking over the scent of the other. So you'll have to either change the litter more often or provide another litterbox.

If you use clumping litter, you won't have to do this chore as often.

can also install boards covered with carpeting that form a ramp all the way up to the ceiling. Attach a wire ladder to a cupboard so that it's secure. Now the cat can make a complete round trip at high altitude.

Scratching Equipment

Various types of scratching equipment are available at the pet store. A scratching tree usually includes parts for climbing and parts for lounging. The trunk is wrapped in sisal, and several elevated seats and snuggling places invite the cat to climb up and relax. You can set up a scratching tree yourself.

Set-up: Glue some carpet onto the main column, a round or square wooden post, cut to fit the height of your room at a lumberyard or garden center. Secure it with angle irons to the floor and wall or ceiling so that it's good and solid. Set up boards covered with carpeting at dif-ferent heights along the post. Between the post and a shelf or windowsill, stretch a thick rope that the cat can balance on; hang up some small balls and other toys, pieces of fur, and colored ribbons.

Location: Place the scratching post in a place where the cat has to pass it on its way to the grooming place or food dish every morning. As the cat scratches on it, it renews its marking.

Note: If you have no room in your home for a scratching post or simply can't find one, attach a space-saving scratching board to the wall or door frame. You could even cover one side of a cabinet with a piece of rug in a spot that your cat passes every day.

Food Dishes

Food dishes should always be placed in the same spot so that your cat can find them whenever it wants. It's a good idea to place them on a plastic place mat. That spares you from cleaning up the surrounding floor. Cats often like to take hunks of food from the dish and eat them from the floor.

From its crow's nest kitty can check the lay of the land without being seen.

Making Your Home Safe for a Cat

Danger	Possible Consequences	Prevention
Balconies and open windows	Falls	Secure with chicken or turkey wire.
Open tip-out windows	Cat can get caught and strangle as it tries to jump through the crack.	Secure with special inserts.
"Caves" such as the drum of a washing machine attract cats.	They quickly get caught in the trap, get pinched, or can suffocate.	Check drawers and cupboard doors before you close them, and washing machine and dryer before turning them on. Cover empty vases.
Doors that the cat can open by jumping on the handle (French doors)	In the case of an outside door, that could lead to some unpleasant surprises.	Replace handle with doorknob, or always keep door locked.
Hot plates, open pots and pans that are sizzling and bubbling, warmers, irons, candles, and burning cigarettes	Curious cats can burn their paws.	Keep pots and pans covered. Unplug or put away irons; extinguish candles and cigarettes.
Needles and pins	The cat can step on them or swallow them.	Don't leave them lying around.
Washing and cleaning agents, chemicals, pills	Poisoning	Everything that's dangerous to children is a hazard to cats; keep it locked up.
Plants such as cyclamen, azalea, dieffenbachia, ivy, hyacinth, philodendron, primrose, poinsettia, and others	Poisoning	Keep these plants out of the cat's reach. Get a complete list from your veterinarian.

What Does a Cat Want?

Your cat will spend hours sleeping in her favorite spot under a blanket on the sofa. Then she'll get up, stretch, and rub against your legs, demanding her tribute of petting. House cats bond closely with their humans in the home and clearly show their affection.

Living with a cat doesn't mean merely acquiring the essentials such as scratching equipment, litterbox, and other things (see Everything the Cat Needs, page 17). In addition to its regular meals, within your four walls kitty has just as great a need for some attention from you: petting, playing, and cuddling. Young cats especially always want to be picked up and to feel your affection. That way you keep them cheerful and happy, and you get pleasure from it. And if cuddling doesn't suit you, you can at least talk nicely to the cat.

Protected by a net, the cat can look out an open window.

What to Expect from a Cat

It's been said that cats live with us, but not for us. You should respect that in your life with the light-footed housemate. When the cat is sleeping, resting, or traveling its mysterious route, it doesn't want to be disturbed. At such times you shouldn't pick it up or try to play with it. It would not react at all, or only grudgingly. But if the impetus to interact with you comes from the cat, it won't leave anyone in peace until you do whatever it wants.

House cats meet many more visitors than do cats that spend a lot of time outside. That doesn't mean, though, that they're always friendly. One cat will lie calmly where she is, but another will disappear until the visitors leave.

Young cats are very curious and can often get themselves into trouble.

What Cats Need to Learn

Usually there are no major problems in training a young cat. It has recently left the mother and has learned from her by example and imitation. In fact, at the time you get a kitten—usually around the age of ten weeks—its behavior is already set in many ways. In contrast to dogs, cats have already completed their socialization phase. Bad habits are hard to eliminate.

VACATION PREPARATION

Leaving the Cat at Home: *Ask your cat-owning friends to recommend a reliable person to come into the house once or twice every day to feed the cat, clean the litterbox, and spend time cuddling and playing. Or ask a friend or neighbor to take care of these chores. Also, professional cat sitters offer their services for hire through classified ads in newspapers.*

Taking the Cat Along: *If you get your cat used to traveling from an early age, you can take the cat with you. See page 31. Continuous changes in vacation destination may be too stressful for a cat. But if you always go to the same vacation house a cat will be glad to go along.*

Boarding the Cat: *If you have friends the cat feels comfortable with, that option will be less stressful for the cat and you. Carefully check out a boarding facility for the cat in advance. All shots will be required (see page 56).*

For example, if a kitten has had no contact with people in the phase that's so sensitive in the socialization process, later on it may always be shy around them. This sensitive phase comprises more or less the first two to seven weeks of life, but neither the beginning nor the end is established precisely. So many kittens that are older than seven weeks can get used to people, even though it may be more difficult for them. In any case, it's better when a kitten is raised by a mother that is friendly with its people, for she transfers that attitude to the youngster. This is one reason why you should have a good look at such details at the breeder's or the cat owner's before you buy a cat (see The Right Cat for You, page 9).

Assuming the cat is well prepared or trained when you get it, you need only reinforce the training in the proper fashion (see HOW-TO: Training, page 50). Remember these points about the cat's behavior:

✔ The kitten has already learned to go to the litterbox and cover up its business. You have to be sure that it can do likewise at your house.

This kitten fell fast asleep in the middle of its playtime.

✔ Scratching with its claws is part of a cat's catalog of natural behaviors. You must place the scratching post in the right location and practice regularly with the kitten.
✔ Sleeping on your bed, jumping onto the table, climbing on the curtains, or begging at the table are bad cat habits that you must oppose with unflagging consistency.

Traveling with Cats

Before the Trip: For a long trip, the night before departure and during the trip you should not give the cat anything to eat so that its digestive system is empty. The excitement of traveling can have a variety of effects, according to my observations. Some cats have to go to the litterbox right away, while others are more at ease.

During the Trip: Provide a plastic pan with kitty litter in a place where it won't move around. Keep a container of water on hand, even if the cat usually drinks little in the hot weather. Let the cat out of the travel cage only when it sits calmly in place.

Be careful in opening windows and doors, and put the cat on a leash (see page 21). Remember that if you intend to cross international borders you'll need the cat's shot records. Get the information you'll need early. You

TIP

Relocating with Your Cat

Help your cat to get used to the new territory, even if, in contrast to the previous residence, you move to an apartment where there is no chance to run free. The cat would suffer a lot more if it were separated from you. Here's what you can do:
✔ If possible, keep the animal in a room emptied beforehand, along with some of its trusted objects (bed, litterbox), until the hubbub of moving is over.
✔ Then take the cat to the new apartment.
✔ Put it in another empty room with its things.
✔ After the apartment is all set up, lead the cat to the new location of the litterbox.
✔ Let the cat explore the new surroundings undisturbed.

can find out what you need to know by consulting your pet store, or the appropriate veterinarian's office.

Traveling by Rail: Sometimes cats can travel free in the coach with you as long as they are in a closed carrier. Check with the railroad first.

Air Travel: On some scheduled flights cats can ride in a travel cage in the cabin. Check first with the airline. Charter organizations usually don't allow cats.

At the Vacation Destination: At your vacation spot stick to the same routine you do at home. If you let your cat outdoors, it might be scared to death and hide in some place you'd never find.

Getting Used to the Car

A few days in advance, set out the travel carrier so that kitty can get acquainted with it. Once the cat has gotten comfortable in the cage, carry it out to the car in the cage while you speak nicely to it. Then bring the cat back into the house. That builds the cat's confidence. The next time, take a short drive, and if the cat survives this stress without reacting in fear, there shouldn't be any further major problems.

Cats and Children

If the kitten is still young, you should show your child the right way to pick it up and carry it, how to pet it (with the lay of the fur, not against it), and how to play with it. Emphasize that the kitten is not to be bathed.

An adult cat can defend itself against overly energetic expressions of love. It simply leaves, or it spits and shows its claws. If you have bought the cat for your child, you must show the youngster how to take care of the animal and feed it, and always to keep an eye on it.

Note: You must never leave a cat alone with a sleeping baby. It might lie on the chest and head of the child, with tragic results.

Established Cats and Newcomers

When my Burmese cat Nina lost her feline companion, she seemed sad and forlorn. So we decided to get a new kitten for her. It was clear that this was not love at first sight. That's a natural reaction, because cats regard the home as their personal property and defend it against other cats (see Cat Meets Cat, page 12). They want nothing to do with a new arrival, even if it's a little kitten. But kittens have youth's lack of inhibition, and you can put that to good use while the two cats are getting used to one another. At first let the new kitten simply explore the home. In the meantime, sit in your usual chair. With the old cat on your lap, pet it, and speak softly to it. That has a calming effect, and the cat may begin to purr. This is a reassuring sound to the newcomer, who will check it out. If the old cat allows the new one to make nose contact, that's a first step.

Usually a little kitten is not frightened away by spitting or a swipe of the paw. It will tag along unconcerned behind the big one, imitating everything it does and challenging it to play with comical jumps. After a while the old cat won't be able to resist this bundle of charm, and will come to appreciate the variety and diversion that have intruded into its life.

Note: Obviously each animal should have its own food dish, and if possible, its own litterbox. That goes for its sleeping place, too, which the cat chooses for itself and will defend.

Cats and children are ideal playmates.

Cats and Dogs

Young Dogs: If both animals are young, they may be too curious and carefree to irritate each other. Each one naturally learns the other's language (see Cats and Other House Pets, page 12). They can live in peace and become friends, but this does not always happen. Some dogs of any age will treat kittens as prey.

Adult Dogs: You can train a well-behaved adult dog to leave a kitten alone.

✔ Keep the two separated until the kitten has made its first journey of exploration in the new surroundings.

✔ Then let the dog in and command it to *"Sit!"* (This assumes a well-trained dog.) The kitten will approach the dog curiously, but will flee at the dog's first movement.

An older cat and a newcomer become friends.

✔ Be sure that the dog does nothing to the kitten. Your dog might even become a defender of the newcomer. Real companionship can grow between the two. But never leave your dog and cat alone together until you are certain they have become friends.

Care: Combing and Brushing

Shorthaired and semilonghaired cats need to be brushed daily so that they don't swallow too much hair when they groom themselves. Stroke the fur energetically with a knobby grooming brush. Don't rub against the lay of the fur, because cats find that unpleasant.

Longhaired cats need to be brushed and combed every day; otherwise their fur becomes

matted. Thoroughly comb the insulating fur, especially on the belly and between the legs, first with a coarse metal comb, and then with a fine-toothed one. Use your fingers to break down a knot of hair into smaller sections, and then comb it out with a metal comb. If that doesn't work, cut it with a seam cutter. Brushing gives the fur its silky sheen. A natural bristle brush or a special brush with curved wire bristles works well.

Note: The fur should be cleaned once a month with a powder that's available in pet stores. Use it sparingly since it dries the skin. Rub the powder in and thoroughly brush it out the next day, brushing evenly against the lay of the hair.

The windowsill is a lookout and a grooming salon for these cats.

Bathing

The tub should be just large enough for the cat to fit in, such as a hand basin. Use a special shampoo recommended by your veterinarian that is effective against fleas and ticks. Put some warm water into the basin, hold the cat securely with one hand on the front paws, and wash the cat with the other hand. Never dunk the cat's head. Rinse the shampoo out carefully and then dry the animal with a warm towel. When you comb the cat, take it onto your lap.

The fur will dry by itself in a warm room. A hair dryer is quicker, but that dulls the fur. A drying brush is what cats like best, and it makes the hair shiny.

Eyes, Ears, and Claws
✔ Remove small crusty deposits from the corners of the eyes with a moistened cotton ball. Always wipe in the direction from ear to nose.
✔ Clean the ears with a cotton ball; don't use cotton swabs! Dark wax clumps and frequent scratching and shaking of the head are signs of ear mites. In that case, visit the veterinarian.

Claw Care: With indoor cats, sometimes the claws don't get worn down enough. Shorten only the translucent tips of the claws that have no blood vessels. You can get a special clipper for this at the pet shop.

Good Nutrition: Variety Without Excess
If a house cat is offered food only in the form of treats, the result is empty calories that put a layer of fat on the animal. So it's important to give the right quantity (see HOW-TO: Feeding, page 38). In deciding how much food is enough, don't rely only on the cat's weight, but on its build. Dainty cats become overweight more quickly than stocky ones.

In addition, a cat that's become used to treats can't easily be switched to any other type of food. Avoid foods that are too fatty, and give the cat a variety of appropriate foods.

Commercial Foods
Commercial foods contain everything that cats need for healthy nutrition. Premium cat foods are specially formulated for every life stage, and you can even find foods for overweight cats and

cats with specific health problems.

Because they are carnivores, cats need protein from animal sources. Their nutritional requirements are unique among mammals. They cannot adapt safely to a vegetarian diet, and they cannot thrive solely on diets designed for humans, dogs, or other animals. Therefore, it's best not to try to give meals that you lovingly prepare yourself. Unless you have the help of a knowledgeable professional such as a veterinarian, it will be extremely difficult and time-consuming to guarantee a nutritionally complete mix of proteins, carbohydrates, fats, vitamins, minerals, and amino acids essential to the feline diet.

For example, taurine, an amino acid, is an essential ingredient found in commercial cat foods. If a cat's food is taurine-deficient, it could develop eye disorders or cardiomyopathy (heart muscle disease).

Other nutritional additives in cat foods include vitamin supplements such as A, D, E, and B-complex, and minerals such as calcium, phosphorus, magnesium, potassium, salt, iron, and zinc. The feline diet requires a delicate balance of these ingredients to maintain proper body functions and cell growth.

The Birman's semilong hair needs to be brushed only occasionally.

Too much or too little of one or the other can be harmful.

Nonnutritional additives include federal Food and Drug Administration-approved artificial and natural preservatives that extend a product's shelf life and artificial coloring that makes the product attractive to the purchaser.

Moist Food comes as a complete diet in cans and consists of a mixture of meat, giblets, or various fish, plus plant protein, grains, minerals, and vitamins. Because of its soft consistency, it doesn't give the cat's teeth and gums much of a workout, and can lead to buildup of tartar and to gum disease. So alternate with harder foods that require more chewing work.

Dry Food is a highly concentrated complete diet that contains only about 10 percent water. Cats need to drink a lot if they are fed dry food. Here's a rule of thumb: provide about 3.5 ounces (100 ml) of water for every 3.5 ounces (100 g) of dry food. Often the quantity of water is not enough to compensate for the long-term fluid deficit. The important thing is to be sure you put out a bowl of fresh water each day.

Most cat owners use the free-choice method, putting down a bowl containing a day's supply of food in the amount recommended by the veterinarian or the food manufacturer. Unlike dogs, which usually wolf as much food as they can at one sitting, most cats take only a little food from time to time, until the bowl is empty.

Your kitten should be offered food about four times a day until it is about six months old. After that, you can use the free-choice method. Exceptions are if your cat is pregnant or lactating. Offer a pregnant queen equal portions of food three or four times a day. If your cat is nursing kittens, give her four to six servings through the fifth week.

Also, elderly or ill cats might need more frequent, smaller feedings. Check with your

Cats eat grass to help them regurgitate the hairs they swallow while grooming themselves.

veterinarian for specially formulated foods and ask about timing your cat's meals.

Foods to Avoid

✔ Don't feed your cat dog food, or let it steal food from your dog's dish. Dog food does not contain enough protein or taurine for a cat's nutritional needs.

✔ Table scraps are okay as occasional treats, but don't let them take the place of cat food specially formulated to maximize your pet's good health. Never feed your cat any scraps that you would not eat.

✔ Don't give your cat bones. They might lodge in the throat or splinter and puncture the gastrointestinal tract.

✔ Don't allow your cat to eat raw meat or fish, which can contain parasites and harmful bacteria. Raw liver can cause vitamin A toxicity.

✔ Chocolate is toxic to cats as well as to dogs.

✔ Alcohol, even in small amounts, can be lethal to your cat.

10 Golden Rules
for Feeding

1 Always feed at the same times, or use the free-choice method (see page 35).

2 Don't keep food sitting out too long. Divide the daily ration into smaller portions and refrigerate portions until you need them. (If you're feeding 4½ ounces [120 g] a day at two meals, give 2¾ ounces [60 g] per meal.)

3 Don't feed cold food straight from the refrigerator. All food should be room temperature.

4 Provide lots of variety, and put down a bowl of fresh water daily.

5 If your cat needs to lose weight, don't make it fast, but rather reduce the portion sizes. Ask your veterinarian about a weight-reduction diet.

6 Don't permit begging between meals (see HOW-TO: Training, page 50).

7 Leftovers from your meals that are given to the cat should not be spicy, salty, or sweet.

8 Rinse out the food dish using only hot water, no cleaning agents.

9 Dog food is not suitable for cats in the long run, because cats need more protein than dogs do.

10 Cats like to relax after eating. Don't play with them at that time.

HOW-TO: FEEDING

How Much a Cat Eats

✔ Up to the age of four to five months a cat can eat up to nearly 9 ounces (250 g) of food a day. Divide the food into two or three meals a day, and don't feed between meals.

✔ Up to the age of seven months a cat eats about 12 ounces (350 g) a day without putting on fat.

✔ Adult indoor cats (with a body weight between 7.75 and 11 pounds or 3.5–5 k) need no more than 4.5 ounces (130 g) spread over two meals. That's about a third of a small can (14 ounces or 400 g), or a quarter-cup of dry food. If the cat is particularly large or very active, the amount of food can be increased to about 5 to 7 ounces (150–200 g).

✔ A pregnant cat should be fed no greater quantities, but the food should be higher in nutritional value and spread out over four or five feedings per day. A nursing cat, on the other hand, needs more food, around 16 ounces (454 g), likewise divided into several meals.

If two cats live together, each should have its own food dish.

Drinks and Drinking Habits

Cats don't drink much, and generally can get enough liquid from their food to satisfy their needs (except for dry food).

Water Always keep a bowl of fresh water on hand.

Milk contains lots of nutrients, such as protein and calcium, and is especially valuable for pregnant and nursing cats as well as young kittens.

Nutrition Essentials

The three ingredients that make up most of the nutritional value of commercial cat food are protein, carbohy-

Kitty washes its face after every meal.

drates, and fat. Small amounts of minerals and vitamins are added—with the exception of vitamin C, which, unlike humans, cats synthesize in adequate amounts in their bodies. Ask your veterinarian and pet store manager about the food that is best formulated for your cat's life stage and activity level.

Protein: The cat is a carnivore, with a need for protein greater than that of the dog, which relishes a more varied banquet. In the wild, cats' source of protein is their prey. Your domesticated house cat, however, must derive its protein from the food you give it. When you read the label on the package, be sure that the food contains a greater percentage of animal protein

What Cats Eat

The following tips and suggestions come from the author's experience. Since each cat reacts differently, you will have to see if your pet likes them.

Practical Feeding Tips

✔ Beef, chicken, pork, veal, lamb, rabbit, or venison must be fresh and come from the best of sources. Serve only meat that you have cooked thoroughly. Cut the meat into cat-sized bites.

✔ Cats need nutritious unseasoned food. Don't add salt or other spices.

✔ A special treat: Mix canned tuna into your cat's dry food occasionally.

✔ If you feed treats as a reward, offer your cat very small pieces of cooked meat or nutritious cat snacks from your pet store.

✔ A teaspoon of mineral oil added to the food once a week helps your cat expel hairballs.

✔ Ask your veterinarian about foods formulated for your cat's age, activity level, and special needs.

The cat eats its food piece by piece.

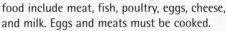

than of any other ingredient. Sources besides commercial food include meat, fish, poultry, eggs, cheese, and milk. Eggs and meats must be cooked.

Carbohydrates: Consisting chiefly of sugar, starches, and cellulose, carbohydrates supply energy and fiber to your cat's diet. Your carnivorous cat's supply of these nutrients will probably come solely from its commercial food; most cats won't touch fruits, vegetables, or even pasta, and are unable to taste sugar.

Fat: For an adult cat of average weight, the fat content of commercial food is sufficient to provide energy and keep your pet's coat sleek and shiny. Buy a food with a lower percentage of fat if your cat needs to lose weight. Kittens and cats that get lots of exercise need foods with higher fat content for energy.

A cat will stand up on its hind legs for a treat.

UNDERSTANDING YOUR INDOOR CAT

Cat language consists of expressive body language and facial expressions that can be supplemented and emphasized by vocalizations.

A Cat's Capabilities

People never tire of marveling at the total suppleness of the feline body: the ease and relaxation in the sleeping position; the stretching and lolling about after waking up; the stalking run wound tight as a coiled spring; the pliant ease with which the cat slips through nooks and crannies; or the acrobatic contortions involved in grooming. The other things cats can do are no less astonishing.

Jumping: A cat can jump five times its own height from a standing position. In so doing, it judges the distance so precisely that it lands right where it wants to. When it jumps down, it bends down so far that it looks like it's running down the wall. It uses this trick to shorten the distance to the floor.

Falling: The ability cats have of always landing on their feet is proverbial. If a cat falls backwards, it spins around lightning fast in mid-air, using its tail as a rudder and a brake, first with the front part of its body, then the rear, arches its back to soften the impact, and usually lands on all fours.

Running: Cats move on silent feet, touching the ground only with their toes. Claws sharp as a needle adorn the silky-soft paws; on the front paws they are retractable. That's why they don't get worn away when the cat walks and they remain sharp.

Balancing: It's fascinating how cats can balance as they walk across a curtain rod. They use their tail much as a tightrope walker uses a pole for balancing.

Sense Perception

The most fascinating thing about cats is their eyes—large amber yellow, copper-colored, violet blue, or emerald green pools. They are not only beautiful, but astonishingly effective as well.

Vision: The size of the eyes allows the cat a kind of panoramic view. In darkness the pupils dilate and collect as much light as possible. The more light there is, the more the pupils contract, until they are reduced to mere slits.

Hearing: Cats hear in frequency ranges up to 65 kHz (people hear only up to 20 kHz) and can perceive such tiny sounds as the squeaking, pitter-patter, and gnawing of mice. Even when

Facial expressions, gestures, and inviting meowing indicate that the kitten is in a mood for play.

they are asleep, they immediately react to strange noises.

Touch: If you cut off a cat's whiskers, it could no longer squeeze through a hole. Cats use these sensitive "antennae" to judge the width of openings and know that they won't get stuck. The whiskers are their navigation system that keeps them from bumping into chair legs in pitch darkness.

Smell: The Jacobson's organ, near the nasal passage, endows the cat with a kind of smell-taste. A cat forms an image of everything by sniffing it. By rubbing with its head, chin, tail, and paws, a cat leaves behind scents that are intelligible only to other cats.

Taste: The sense of taste may not be as highly developed in cats as in other animals. They stick with a particular food probably because they like the smell of it. They can distinguish between salted and unsalted foods, but they have no particular taste for sweets. Just the same, they will swipe a cream-filled pastry from the table simply because they can't resist the opportunity.

A Cat's Instinctive Behavior

✔ Purring expresses more than contentment. It's more indicative of "I'm in a peaceful frame of mind." The meaning can change according to situation and social conditions. Mother cats purr while they are nursing and grooming the little ones. Kittens purr when they want to invite grown cats or people to play. Friendly cats purr at every meeting. Dominant cats purr when they approach subordinate ones peacefully. Sick and very weak cats purr for comfort.

✔ Kneading: The cat sits on your lap and presses down slowly and regularly with alternate front paws. Baby kittens use this kneading to stimulate milk flow in the mother. Grown cats are therefore repeating a juvenile behavior pattern, and feel themselves ill-served if they are rejected.

✔ Licking: A cat licks itself several times a day to clean itself. Sometimes it merely gives itself a quick once-over on the nose or the fur even where there is nothing to clean off.

✔ Rubbing: When a cat greets you it rubs closely around your legs. When its forehead, cheeks, flanks, and tail rub against a person's legs, the cat is exchanging body scents with you. It has perfumed you with the scent glands that are located in the temples, the corners of the mouth, and the root of the tail. Since cats afterward groom themselves very thoroughly, they also take in your scent with their tongue.

✔ Scratching: One of the reasons the cat claws your favorite chair is to mark it with its scent (see Opportunities to Scratch, page 23). Cats have scent glands on the bottom of their feet that are rubbed forcibly on the furniture when they scratch. That's how they add their scent to

Cats move with incomparable suppleness and speed.

Behavior Problems

If your cat suddenly starts doing things that it never did before, you naturally will become perplexed. Problems of this type can appear out of the blue in a previously well-trained cat, and can fundamentally disrupt your harmonious life together. Even cats that you've adopted from the humane society and that have been great for weeks can take a sharp turn for the worse. Before you undertake drastic measures, you should know that such reactions almost always

yours and express their affection. So if they ignore the scratching apparatus you've provided for them, it sometimes helps to drape a discarded tee-shirt over it.

The cat snoozes with half-closed eyes, but its ears are still attuned to any noise.

have a cause that can be corrected. If you can't speak to a previous owner, observe your pet to learn what is behind its change in behavior.

Inappropriate Eliminations

If your cat suddenly begins depositing messes on your carpet, there can be several causes.

Illness or Old Age: In this case the cat should be taken to the veterinarian right away.

Litterbox: It needs to be cleaned; it's placed in the wrong location, such as near the eating dish, or it has been set up in a part of the home that people continually pass by.

BODY LANGUAGE

If you want to learn cat language, you must correctly interpret your animal's behavior.

 My cat exhibits this behavior.

? *What is my cat trying to tell me?*

! *The right way to react to this behavior.*

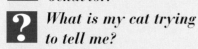

The cat gets up, yawns, and stretches with gusto.

? It is rested and ready for new activity.

! Let it go about its business.

The cat rubs against your legs.

? It's making contact with you.

! Pet the cat and talk to it.

Pupils are dilated and the cat is hissing and spitting.

The cat is very agitated. **?**

Leave it alone or you will **!** feel its claws.

The kitten is relaxed and sleeping.

? It's tired and needs to rest.

! Don't disturb it.

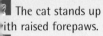 The cat rubs its head on someone's forehead.

It's in a good mood and is looking for attention.

Now's a good time to snuggle with it.

Two kittens romp clumsily with each other.

They are practicing defensive and aggressive moves by playing.

Don't interfere, and let the two kittens finish their wrestling match.

The cat stands up with raised forepaws.

Its predatory urge has been stimulated.

Throw it a little ball to play with.

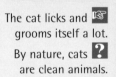 The cat licks and grooms itself a lot.

By nature, cats are clean animals.

Keep the litterbox clean.

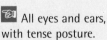 All eyes and ears, with tense posture.

The cat is alert and interested.

Let it make a grab for a toy.

TIP

Nibbling on Plants

Cats, especially longhaired ones, need greens–probably to help them regurgitate the hairs they swallow when they groom. Set out a pot of wheat or oat grass just for the cat–far away from your houseplants– and get it used to it in good time. Praise the cat when it eats its grass, and say "No!" if it attacks your plants. Don't shout, or you'll frighten your cat and it won't trust you.

Often cats nibble out of pure boredom; for example, if they have to spend the whole day alone. Provide more variety (see HOW-TO: Living Space, pages 26–27), and protect your plants (e.g., with moth balls in small bags) or keep harmful plants out of the cat's reach.

Disruption of the Usual Routine: This is one of the most common causes of uncleanliness. Strange people have created a disturbance; new furniture has interfered with the accustomed territory; or another cat has arrived on the scene. Strengthen the cat's confidence, and at the same time clean up the "piddle place" by spraying with mint or lemon oil. Or try a commercial cleaner that dissolves the enzymes in urine, eliminating most of the odor. Scolding or clapping your hands serves no purpose and will upset your cat.

Yarn should not be rolled too tightly. Kittens could get tangled up in it and even injure themselves.

Note: Cleaning products that contain ammonia have a smell like urine and stimulate the cat to deposit more scent.

Avoiding the Scratching Post

Wrong Place: Since the cat doesn't pass by the scratching post on its way through the house, it has chosen a different place to scratch. Remove the abused piece of furniture and put the scratching post in its place.

Cover the scratched spot with a slippery sheet of plastic, and put the scratching post close by. Dangle a small toy or cloth sack filled with catnip from the post to entice the cat.

Learning too late: You may have made the scratching post available after the cat had already formed its habit. Now you must get it to change the habit.

Aggressive Cats

Perhaps you have taken in a stray cat, or one from an animal shelter, that has had some bad experiences in its life. It is bound to have some aggressive tendencies. On the other hand, if a cat you've had since it was a normal kitten suddenly develops the habit of scratching and biting visitors, you must determine the cause.

Jealousy: If you were formerly single and now have a new partner, the cat may not like it. Have the new person feed the cat and pet it, while you hold back. With time the cat probably will take to the newcomer.

Fear: When cats come to the end of their rope, they hiss, scratch, and bite. Remove the cause of the fear, and they will once again be the usual gentle, cuddly creatures.

Sucking

When a newly acquired little kitten sucks on your finger, you may find it cute. But if a grown cat sucks on fabric, wool, hair, or your ear, you should do something about it. Push the cat away as soon as it starts to suck. If it won't stop, say "No!" and give it one of its toys to distract it. Be consistent in your refusal, or your attempts will come to naught.

Cats Need to Play

In playing, cats practice behaviors that they will need later on: stalking, lurking, pursuing, grabbing, biting, and pouncing on their prey. House cats don't need to hunt, but the skills survive and lie dormant if the cat has nothing at its disposal to satisfy this urge. So playing with a cat is an important part of creating a satisfying life for it.

Balancing

A treat provides an incentive for a cat to go from one chair to another by walking along a broom handle. Lure the cat with a morsel, and when it has negotiated the broom handle, praise it and reward it. Once it has mastered the performance, it will do it even without the treat.

Hiding

Nothing stimulates the former cave-dwelling cat as much as hiding in a dark hole. Set up an

The scratching post must not wobble, or the cat will have nothing more to do with it.

unfolded newspaper on the floor like a roof and rattle it alluringly. The cat won't hesitate to investigate the matter. Even an empty box is of great interest, especially if the opening is just a crack.

Rolling

Cats love big, empty plastic buckets. Clean them out thoroughly and cover them with carpet remnants so that kitty can claw them. The dark hole invites the cat to crawl inside. The cat can also roll around with it, jump on it and over it, and play hide-and-seek with another

cat. When a cat is inside you can scratch lightly on the outside and add to the excitement.

Cats get ready for real life when they play at pursuit and defense.

Playing Ball

Give your cat a hard rubber ball with a surface that's not too slick. Soft foam rubber balls are not a good choice because cats tear them apart and eat them. A cat will run after a ball, throw it high over its shoulder with a deft movement of the paw, pull it back lightning-fast, chase it again, and pounce on it for the kill.

Crawling and Chasing

Crawl on all fours. Your cat will be waiting for you around the next corner. Outwardly calm, it sits wide-eyed, with only the tip of its tail twitching in excitement. At the next instant the cat bolts away and you must follow.

But only as far as the next chair, because now it's the cat's turn to stalk the enemy. Go behind a door and wait. Your cat will probably come looking for you. When it senses you are hiding, dash out and run for it! Your cat will chase you, then might leap on top of the piano or the refrigerator and watch like a leopard on a tree branch.

Training Your Cat

Dogs live to please. Cats do not. Don't try to train your cat in the same way you would train your dog. This does not mean you cannot teach your cat to do some things on command—if

Most cats love to play with catnip and roll around in it. Pet stores have a variety of catnip toys.

there is something in it for him or her. It takes longer to train an adult than it does a kitten, because the adult has become set in its ways, while the kitten is more receptive to stimuli that help it learn.

The first thing to teach your cat is its own name. Say its name over and over when playing with it and whenever you are near it and have its attention. Once the cat recognizes its name you can begin to train it to come when called.

Come When Called

Most cats respond to the sound of the can opener at dinnertime. While your cat is still a kitten or an adult cat just becoming accustomed to the ways of your household, call its name each time you open a can of cat food. If you feed dry food, rattle the bag loudly and call your cat's name. After two weeks of this, start calling your cat at other times, and rewarding it with a small treat each time it responds. After your cat has come when called for two weeks without backsliding, and been rewarded with a treat each time, start giving it a treat every other time, then less frequently, until it will come on command without any reward. You'll have to give it an occasional treat as reinforcement, however, or your cat will lose interest and regress to responding only when it hears the can opener or rattling food bag.

Cats have a mind of their own and can't be forced to do anything they don't want to. Kittens learn by imitation. They observe their mother and imitate what she does. Now you have to take over her role. Setting an example is the only sensible approach to training young cats. With an older cat that has lived a long time according to its own laws, training consists of setting limits so that kitty stops its undesirable behavior.

Five Training Rules

1. Always speak softly to the cat. It will do what you want only when it trusts you.
2. Be consistent in your demands. If you forbid begging at the table today, don't feed it treats tomorrow.
3. Don't yell. Say "No!" firmly if the cat is scratching the

A scratching post will keep your cat from tearing the upholstery.

Scratching

The cat must learn to scratch its claws on the scratching post, board, or carpet provided for that purpose; otherwise it will misuse your furnishings. As soon as you see that it's contemplating scratching on the chair or the carpet, bring it to its scratching apparatus. Show it what it must do by drawing its paws back and forth on the rough surface. Repeat that a few times until the cat gets the idea.

With a little kitten, pawing means that it has to go.

armchair again, rather than the scratching board. Don't call the cat loudly by name to stop it.
4. Be consistent. Always use the same expressions such as "No!" "Down!" or "Off!"
5. Praise immediately. Pat the cat or reward it if it has obeyed you. Don't speak harshly to it, or it will simply ignore you next time.

Cleanliness

A young kitten usually comes already housebroken. Now you have to get it used to the new place for the litterbox. As soon as it meows and looks around, quickly place the cat in the litterbox. Then praise the cat. If that doesn't work right away, you have to keep a close eye on the cat and try to seize the right moment. Always praise it generously when it goes into the box. Use a squirt bottle to deliver a quick correction if you catch it in the act of doing something wrong. Squirting it after an accident has occurred is pointless and will not help to train the cat.

Breaking Bad Habits

A sudden stream of water from a squirt bottle, a sharp blast of air from a bellows, or the toss of a small aluminum chain are actions that when used properly can frighten and serve as a deterrent. If your cat climbs up the drapes, claws your best armchair, or jumps onto the kitchen table where you have unpacked your groceries, an unpleasant surprise is effective. Be sure that you catch the cat in the act and deploy the stream of water or the aluminum chain without saying a word. The cat must not be ready for it or associate you with the negative stimulus. Specifically, if it notices that the fright that's sprung on it originates with you, it will lose confidence in you. Trust is the basis for effective training. It's always more effective, for example, to toss the chain at the start of the undesirable behavior. Here's another important point: So that chain or bottle doesn't lose its magical effect, the cat should hear the rattling or feel the spray only at the instant the offense is committed, and not at any other time.

The unexpected shower from the plant sprayer must catch the cat in the act.

Begging at the Table

✔ A cat that continually begs during meals is a nuisance. To break it of the habit, you must be absolutely consistent.

✔ Give it a little food in its dish when you sit down to eat.

✔ Keep it from coming closer with a clear "No!" if it approaches the table.

✔ If it jumps onto your lap during the meal, set it back onto the floor with the command *"Down!"*

✔ Under no circumstances must you get carried away and give the cat anything to eat. If you do so even once, all your previous efforts will be in vain and you will have a regular guest at your table.

You can give the cat a little food in its dish while you are eating.

HEALTH CONSIDERATIONS AND ILLNESSES

Cats are reputed to be tougher and more resistant to illness than many other animals. You can contribute to this desirable situation by providing what your cat needs and giving it a balanced diet and loving care.

Immunizations Are the Best Prevention

Vaccinations are the most important and most effective preventive health measure for your cat. The animal must be healthy and free of parasites in order to be vaccinated. Have a stool sample examined by the veterinarian before you have the cat immunized. The veterinarian will maintain a record of the immunizations and keep track of when booster shots are needed (see Immunization Schedule, page 56).

Panleukopenia: This very infectious viral illness is transmitted not only from animal to animal, but also through carriers, and even by hands, shoes, and other objects.

Feline Respiratory Illness: This is the most common illness, especially among young cats. Cats that have been immunized can also become ill, but less so than unvaccinated ones.

Leukemia: Also known as Feline Leukemia. It's transmitted from cat to cat (through biting, licking, and mating). It's detectable with a test performed by a veterinarian.

Rabies: This is communicable to humans (see page 54). Vaccination (and sometimes quarantine) is required for crossing international borders.

Feline Infectious Peritonitis (FIP): Also known as inflammation of the peritoneum. The blood test and immunization for FIP are controversial. Get advice from your veterinarian.

Note: There are no shots for Aujeszky's Disease and feline AIDS. The feline immunodeficiency virus (FIV) belongs to the same group of viruses as the AIDS pathogen in humans, but it is not dangerous to us. So you don't need to get rid of your cat if FIV is detected. Follow your veterinarian's advice.

Worming

A young kitten usually has no worms if its mother is free of worms. The veterinarian is the only one who can determine this, so you should bring a stool sample when it's time to have the cat vaccinated. If necessary, the veterinarian will administer worm medicine (preparations in paste or tablet form). In the case of house cats, which are not likely to become reinfested easily, the worming treatment will not need to be repeated.

With its alert bearing and clear eyes, this cat projects an image of good health.

Illnesses Communicable to Humans

An indoor cat that has been vaccinated and eats only home-cooked or commercial foods seldom picks up pathogens that are also dangerous to humans.

Rabies: Laws regarding frequency of vaccination vary from state to state and across international borders. Check with your veterinarian. If you plan to travel with your cat outside the country, consult a veterinarian or the country's consulate.

Toxoplasmosis is spread through contact with infected cat feces. This disease is very dangerous for pregnant women, because it can produce severe damage to the brain and eyes of unborn children. Women should advise their

Symptoms of illness are readily apparent in a cat that's well cared for.

doctor that they are cat owners as soon as they become pregnant and have their blood checked for toxoplasmosis. Ask your doctor how often your blood should be tested.

Note: Throughout the length of your pregnancy, avoid close physical contact with your cat, and have someone else clean out the litterbox. It's not at all necessary to get rid of your cat. It would be cruel of you to relinquish your pet just because you're afraid of becoming infected.

Microsporum: This is caused by a skin fungus and is evidenced by hair loss and continual scratching. For treatment you must consult the veterinarian. Everything that the cat has come into contact with—bed, comb, brush, and toys—must be disinfected to prevent reinfection. Sometimes things must simply be thrown away. Wash your hands carefully after every time you touch your cat.

When a Cat Becomes Ill

A *healthy cat* is lively, curious, and playful, and it grooms regularly and frequently from the time it's small. Further signs of its well-being are thick, shiny fur, clear eyes, clean ears (inside, too), healthy teeth with no tartar, pink gums with no unpleasant odor, soft, dark, well-formed droppings, and clear, yellow urine.

A *sick cat* sits around listlessly, doesn't eat, and scratches itself frequently. Further indications that point to a health disorder or illness include continual thirst, diarrhea, more vomiting than usual, fever, coughing, and severe loss of weight. In such cases you must not put off visiting the veterinarian.

A Trip to the Veterinarian

Since you will have to go to the veterinarian at least once a year for preventive shots, you should find a professional who knows cats and whom you can trust.

✔ Carry the cat in a travel cage or kennel. Most veterinarians require that cats be confined while in the waiting room.

✔ Briefly describe the symptoms and answer clearly any questions the veterinarian may have. You may need to bring a stool sample.

What the Cat Owner Can Do

Cats are not particularly patient patients, and it won't occur to your cat that the treatment is in its best interest. So you may have to resort to all kinds of tricks.

Checklist
Health Check

1 Fur is clean, smooth, and free of knots and tangles.

2 Eyes are clear and shiny; there should be no discharge or abnormalities present.

3 The nose is dry and warm, but not hot.

4 The ears are completely clean inside. Shaking the head or holding the head at an angle are indications of mite infestation.

5 The anal region must be clean. Uncleanliness is a sign of diarrhea.

6 The skin must be free of parasites and skin diseases. Continuous scratching of specific spots is a clear indication that something is wrong with the skin.

Immunization Schedule for Good Health

	Age	Panleukopenia	Respiratory Illnesses	Leukemia	Rabies	Calcivirus
Basic Immuni-zations	6–8 weeks	●	●			●
	10–12 weeks	●	●	●	●	●
	16 weeks	●	●	●		●
	yearly	●	●	●	●*	●

Note: Get advice about these and other immunizations from your veterinarian—particularly rabies. *Regulations regarding frequency of vaccination against rabies vary from state to state.

If the veterinarian prescribes medicine, stick closely to the recommended dosage, and keep giving the medicine until it is finished. Carefully follow any other instructions given by the veterinarian.

Sick Bed: Place a soft cushion into a shallow box or cat bed, and on top of that a cloth that can be washed when it's changed.

Location: A warm, draft-free place where you can comfortably take care of the patient. If you have other cats, keep the sick one isolated if it has an infectious illness.

Feeding: Fresh, warmed delicacies, or tasty concentrated food available from the veterinarian. If it's hard for the cat to chew, puree the chunks of food. Sometimes the cat will need to be fed by hand. Slowly dribble chicken broth behind the canine teeth, using a syringe (with needle removed). Don't spray in a stream, or the cat may choke.

Drinking: Fresh drinking water must always be available.

Tablets, Pills, and Capsules: Hide them in a tasty morsel of food; divide large pills into smaller pieces and put them into several treats. If your cat refuses to eat such morsels, try the following: Hold the pill ready between the thumb and forefinger of one hand and with

the other, lightly grasp the cat's head behind the teeth. The cat will involuntarily open its mouth. Place the pills as far as possible into the throat and gently massage the throat downwards until you feel the pill go down.

Taking the Temperature: This is easier if there are two people. One holds the cat firmly by the shoulders and forepaws, while the other lifts the tail a little and inserts the lubricated thermometer into the anus. Digital thermometers register the temperature after one minute; conventional ones, after two minutes. The normal temperature is between 100 and 102.6°F (37.8°–39.2°C).

Taking the Pulse: This works best on the inside of the thigh; normal pulse rate is between 110 and 140 beats per minute.

Eye Salves: Hold the cat's head securely from behind at the same time you carefully draw back the upper eyelid with the forefinger. Put down a bead of salve about a ¼-inch (5 mm) long under the lid. Never touch the eyeball directly with the tip of the tube!

Eye and Ear Drops: Hold the cat's head securely from behind and carefully pull down the lower eyelid with your index finger as you dribble the drops into the eye. Use the dropper to drip two or three drops behind the lid. Never touch the eyeball directly!

When you put drops into the ears, carefully pull up the outer ear and introduce four or five drops into the ear canal. Then gently massage the base of the ear to distribute the fluid into the auditory canal.

Injections: A diabetic cat must have a daily injection. Have the veterinarian show you how to do it. When you've had some practice, the cat will scarcely feel it, and might even present the "shot spot" to you at the appointed time.

Note: With some procedures you can wrap the cat up in a large towel so that it can't scratch you.

Treating Minor Illnesses

If your cat is sick, you should get quick and professional help from a veterinarian. But

there are some treatments you can administer. For example, natural remedies are available in pharmacies or health food stores. But don't waste time in trial and error where your pet's health is concerned. Ask your veterinarian first.

Mild Diarrhea: Immediately eliminate inappropriate food (milk, raw liver, spoiled meat). If there is no improvement after two days, take the cat to the veterinarian.

Mild Constipation: Longhaired cats often experience this. Frequently a little milk or one to two teaspoonfuls of olive oil added to the meal will act as a laxative. If two days have passed without a bowel movement, or if the cat is vomiting, take the cat to the veterinarian.

Respiratory Illness: Chamomile vapors (with concentrated chamomile from the drug store) can help. Place the cat in its travel cage in front of the container of steaming chamomile, or hold the cat on your lap under a towel. If the condition doesn't improve within 12 hours, take the cat to the veterinarian.

Inflammation of the Eyes: If lids are swollen, carefully treat the corners of the eyes three to four times a day with euphrasia (ten drops in a glass of lukewarm water). Take the animal to the veterinarian if there is no improvement within 48 hours.

Superficial Injuries: Dress or salve with tincture of calendula or a chamomile tincture.

Treating Shock After an Accident: One of the most important life-saving first aid measures. Have someone call the veterinarian

Little kittens can easily become sick, so preventive measures are vitally important.

immediately while you lay the cat on its right side (as long as there's no external injury) on a blanket or towel, wrap it up, and place the animal gently into its bed or on your lap. Keep the head lower than the body so that the brain remains supplied with blood. Take the cat to the veterinarian immediately.

Emergency Readiness

The key to coping with any emergency is to be prepared. Always keep your veterinarian's phone number handy. Tape it to your phones or secure it to your refrigerator door with a magnet. Assemble the following items in a first-aid kit.

✔ A blanket or towel to wrap your cat in for warmth and safe restraint
✔ Gauze pads and strips for bandaging
✔ Peroxide to clean wounds and—after consulting your veterinarian—to induce vomiting
✔ Antibiotic ointment for superficial cuts and scrapes
✔ Tweezers for removing ticks or for extracting foreign objects from between the pads or from the throat if cat is choking
✔ Jar of alcohol; drop tick into it to kill it
✔ Ice pack to control swelling or bleeding
✔ Scissors
✔ Adhesive tape
✔ Artificial tears or saline solution to wash foreign objects from eyes
✔ Pediatric-size rectal thermometer

A kitten learns everything it needs in life by imitating its mother.

Elderly Cats

Old cats don't necessarily have to suffer from ill health. Change as little as possible in the cat's surroundings, and have your pet checked every three to four months by the veterinarian. It may suffer from constipation, dental problems, and reduced acuity of hearing and vision.

Euthanizing a Cat: If the cat is sick and in great pain, you should consult with the veterinarian to see if euthanasia is the best solution. Hold the cat lovingly in your arms; it will feel nothing more than a small pinprick, and then pass away peacefully.

Kittens are interested in anything that moves

60 I N D E X

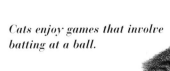

*Cats enjoy games that involve
batting at a ball.*

Addresses

Cat Associations

American Association of Cat
  Enthusiasts (AACE)
P.O. Box 213
Pine Brook, NJ 07058
(201) 335-6717

American Cat
  Association (ACA)
8101 Katherine Avenue
Panorama City, CA 91402
(818) 781-5656

American Cat Fanciers
  Association (ACFA)
Dept. CF
P.O. Box 203
Pt. Lookout, MO 65726
(417) 334-5430

Canadian Cat
  Association (CCA)
220 Advance Boulevard
  Suite 101
Brampton, Ontario
Canada L6T 4J5
(905) 459-1481

Cat Magazines

Cats
2 News Plaza
P.O. Box 1790
Peoria, IL 61656
(309) 682-6626

Cat Fancy
P.O. Box 6050
Mission Viejo, CA 92690
(714) 855-8822

Cat Fancier's Almanac
P.O. Box 1005
Manasquan, NJ 08736-0805
(908) 528-9797
Catnip (newsletter)

Tufts University School of
  Veterinary Medicine
P.O. Box 420014
Palm Coast, FL 32142-0014
(800) 829-0926

Books

Behrend, K. *Cats.* Hauppauge,
  New York: Barron's
  Educational Series, Inc., 1999.
Behrend, K. and Wegler, Monika.
  *The Complete Book of Cat
  Care.* Hauppauge, New York:
  Barron's Educational Series,
  Inc., 1991.
Daly, Carol Himsel, D.V.M.
  Caring for Your Sick Cat.
  Hauppauge, New York:
  Barron's Educational Series,
  Inc., 1994
Frye, Fredric. *First Aid for Your
  Cat.* Hauppauge, New York:
  Barron's Educational Series,
  Inc., 1993.
Maggitti, Phil. *Guide to a Well-
  Behaved Cat.* Hauppauge,
  New York: Barron's
  Educational Series, Inc., 1993
Head, Honor. *101 Questions Your
  Cat Would Ask.* Hauppauge,
  New York: Barron's
  Educational Series, Inc., 1999.
Viner, Bradley, D.V.M. *The
  Cat Care Manual.* Hauppauge,
  New York: Barron's Educa-
  tional Series, Inc., 1993

The Author
Katrin Behrend, a journalist, animal book editor, and author of pet books, lives in Munich, Germany, and in Italy. She has owned cats for many years.

The Illustrator
Renate Holzner works as a freelance illustrator. Her style encompasses everything from line drawings to photorealistic illustrations and computer graphics.

Photographers
Animal Photography/Thompson: pages 2–3; Cogis/Gengoux: pages 4–5; Gissey: page 37 (large photo); Cogis/Lanceau: page 29 bottom; Juniors: pages 12, 57; Juniors/Aschermann: page 14 bottom, 22, 43; Juniors/Bohle: pages 29 top, 59; Juniors/Born: pages 8, 34, 39 top; Juniors/Caspersen: pages 46, 54; Juniors/Heidtmann: pages 6–7, 10, 33, 58; Juniors/Liebold: pages 35, 42; Juniors/Pinkeert-Enger: page 25; Juniors/Putz: page 44 left middle; Juniors/Schanz: pages 11, 14 top right, 15 lower left, 17, 19, 24, 36, 37 (small photo), 38 top, 40, 47, 48, 55, 61, 64; Juniors/Sock: page 52; Juniors/Wegler: pages 30–31, 39 bottom, 45 right middle; Juniors/Wegner: pages 9, 18, 23; Reinhard: pages 44 right middle, 53; Schanz: pages 14 left middle, right middle, 15 top left, top right, left middle, 32, 38 bottom, 41, 45 top left, top right, bottom left, bottom right, 49; Schneider/Will: page 44, top right, 44 bottom; Wegler: page 15 right middle.

Important Note
Be sure that your cat has all its important shots and is wormed (see pages 53 and 56); otherwise there is health danger for humans and animal. Some illnesses and parasites are communicable to humans (see page 54). Therefore, you should consult a veterinarian if your cat shows symptoms of illness (see page 57). In questionable cases, consult your doctor and report that you own a cat. Some people are allergic to cat hair. If you are not sure, find out from your doctor before you get a cat. You may get bitten or scratched in your dealings with a cat. Have such injuries immediately treated by a doctor. Your cat may damage others' property or cause accidents. Therefore adequate insurance coverage is in your own interest; in any case you should carry liability insurance.

The Translator
Eric A. Bye, M.A., a cat owner, works in German, French, Spanish, and English at his office in Vermont.

Cover Photo
Front cover: Norvia Behling

English translation copyright © 1999 by Barron's Educational Series, Inc.
Original title of the book in German is *Wohnungskatzen*
Copyright © 1998 Grafe und Unzer Verlag GmbH, Munich

Translation from the German by Eric A. Bye

All inquiries should be addressed to:
Barron's Educational Series, Inc.
250 Wireless Boulevard
Hauppauge, NY 11788
http://www.barronseduc.com
Library of Congress Catalog Card No. 99-19207
ISBN-13: 978-0-7641-0935-5
ISBN-10: 0-7641-0935-9

Library of Congress Cataloging-in-Publication Data
Behrend, Katrin.
[Wohnungskatzen. English]
Indoor cats / Katrin Behrend ; illustrations by Renate Holzner ; [translated from the German by Eric A. Bye].
p. cm. — (Complete pet owner's manual)
Includes bibliographical references (p.   ) and index.
ISBN 0-7641-0935-9
1. Cats. 2. Cats—Behavior. I. Title. II. Series.
SF447.B4613   1999
636.8—dc21   99-19207
CIP

Printed in China
19 18 17 16 15 14 13 12 11

1 Do cats miss their freedom if they're kept inside and don't run free?

If cats have never been permitted to run free, they have no sense of what it's like and don't feel the lack of it.

2 Can being kept inside for a long time lead to problems?

That's likely only if the cat is bored in the house or apartment and you don't give it the necessary attention (see page 47).

3 Should a person get one or two cats?

Two cats play, cuddle, and romp together and keep each other active. However, they may not always get along.

4 Does a cat suffer if it moves from a home where it can run free into an apartment?

Not really. It will suffer, though, if you give it away just so it can stay in a home where it can run free—because it will miss you.

5 Does a person need the landlord's permission to own a cat?

Yes. The landlord usually has to give consent (see page 16).

An expert answers the ten most common questions about indoor cats.